P9-BZA-084

VERTEBRATES

VERTEBRATES

DR. ALVIN, VIRGINIA, AND ROBERT SILVERSTEIN

TWENTY-FIRST CENTURY BOOKS

A Division of Henry Holt and Company

New York

Twenty-First Century Books
A Division of Henry Holt and Company, Inc.
115 West 18th Street
New York, NY 10011

Henry Holt® and colophon are trademarks of
Henry Holt and Company, Inc.
Publishers since 1866

Published in Canada by Fitzhenry & Whiteside Ltd.
195 Allstate Parkway, Markham, Ontario L3R 4T8

Library of Congress Cataloging-in-Publication Data
Silverstein, Alvin.
Vertebrates / Alvin Silverstein, Virginia Silverstein, and Robert Silverstein. — 1st ed.
p.   cm. — (The Kingdoms of life)
Includes index.
Summary: Describes the subphylum of animals with backbones.
1. Vertebrates—Juvenile literature. [1. Vertebrates.] I. Silverstein, Virginia B. II. Silverstein, Robert A.
III. Title. IV. Series: Silverstein, Alvin. The Kingdoms of life.
QL605.3.S54 1996   95–45672
596—dc20   CIP
                                                                                     AC

ISBN 0–8050–3517–6
First Edition 1996

Designed by Kelly Soong

Printed in the United States of America
All first editions are printed on acid-free paper ∞.
10 9 8 7 6 5 4 3 2 1

Photo credits

CONTENTS

THE KINGDOMS OF LIFE

ANIMALS

Great horned owl

VERTEBRATES

Day octopus

INVERTEBRATES

PLANTS

Silver vase

FUNGI

Hygrophorus mushroom

MONERANS

Cyanobacteria

PROTISTS

Diatoms

VERTEBRATES

1

OUR LIVING WORLD

CLASSIFYING PEOPLE

How many people do you know? If you try to make a list of them, you may find that you are using various groupings to recall more names. Some are children, and some are adults. Some of the children are boys, and some are girls; the adults can also be divided into men and women. Some of the people on your list are relatives, some are friends, and some are just acquaintances. Your relatives include very close relatives (brothers, sisters, parents) and more distant ones (grandparents, aunts and uncles, cousins). You may also classify the people you know in other ways—on the basis of physical characteristics (tall and short; or blonds, brunettes, and redheads) or according to how much you like or dislike them.

There are more than five billion people in the world today, but we humans are just a tiny fraction of all the life on earth. We share our planet with uncountable numbers of other living things. Can you imagine how many trees there are? How many fish? How many flies?

Each living creature is an individual, but it is similar in a number of ways to many others. A cat and a dog, for example, both have four legs, two ears, and two eyes. Both eat mainly meat and like to live with people. But any two cats are much more alike than a cat and a dog. And even though cats and dogs can learn to like each other and live contentedly in the same house, they would never mate.

People have always been interested in the living creatures around them and curious about their relationships. Some distinctions are very important—an ancient hunter who spotted an animal in the woods, for instance, needed to know quickly whether the animal was likely to be good to eat or something that liked to eat people! So people have observed the other creatures of the earth very closely and have tried to find patterns in their similarities and differences, to trace the relationships among them—to classify them.

CLASSIFICATION SORT OF SORTS

Carl Linnaeus (1707–1778) devised the scientific method of naming living things. He wrote books in Latin on the classification of plants and animals.

Classification is the process of dividing objects into related groups. An object—such as an animal, a rock, or a star—is identified, described, and placed into a group with other, similar objects. This helps people to identify that object and understand how it is related to other objects.

Taxonomy is the science of classifying or arranging living things into groups based on characteristics they share. It comes from the Greek words *taxis*, which means "arrangement," and *nomos*, which means "law."

Early humans distinguished between nonliving things, such as rocks and water, and living things. The differences between plants and animals also seemed obvious. Plants were living things that were usually green, made their own food, and did not move around on their own. Animals seemed more active and complex; they could move, perceive and react to their surroundings, and had to eat to get nourishment for their growth and activities. Through the ages, people continued to find patterns in the kingdoms of life, and classification schemes gradually developed. But they were often very complicated and confusing. The modern science of taxonomy dates back to the work of an eighteenth-century Swedish naturalist and botanist, Carl Linnaeus.

LINNAEUS AND THE TWO-NAME SYSTEM

WHAT'S IN A NAME?

An organism's *first* name tells a lot about how it is related to other living things. But very different organisms could have the same *second* name and have little in common. If you went to a restaurant that listed food items by their scientific names, some people would love to order *Homarus americanus* (Atlantic lobster). But *Bufo americanus* wouldn't be such a treat—that is the scientific name for the American toad!

Linnaeus divided animals and plants into groups according to their structure. He gave scientific names to each **species**, or kind of organism. He also assigned each species a specific place in his classification system.

Linnaeus's system is called **binomial nomenclature** (which means "two-name naming") because each type of organism is given two names, a genus name and a species name. The genus name is like a person's last name because it includes the type of organism in a larger group. The genus name always begins with a capital letter, but unlike our last names, it comes first in the organism's name. The species name follows the genus name and begins with a lowercase letter.

MEMORY AIDS

Silly sentences can help you remember lists such as the groupings of the scientific classification system. For example, the first letters of

Keep **P**enguins **C**ool **O**r **F**ind **G**ood **S**helter

can help you remember

Kingdom, **P**hylum, **C**lass, **O**rder, **F**amily, **G**enus, **S**pecies.

The scientific name is usually italicized or underlined. It is made up of Latin (and sometimes Greek) words. Scientists all around the world use the same name for any type of organism, no matter what language they normally use. For example, a large member of the cat family is known in various parts of North America and South America as cougar, mountain lion, panther, and puma, but its scientific name is *Felis concolor*.

From an organism's scientific name a person can easily figure out how that organism fits into the classification system because, as Charles Darwin said, Linnaeus "grouped his groups." He placed similar genera into larger groups called orders. Then he placed orders with similarities into classes.

As scientists expanded Linnaeus's system, other groupings were added. Our modern taxonomic system is made up of seven groupings: kingdom, phylum, class, order, family, genus, and species.

Kingdoms are the largest groups, whose members share only a few basic characteristics in common. For a long time, people divided the living world into just two

Mountain lion

kingdoms, animals and plants. But now most biologists recognize five kingdoms of life: monerans (bacteria), protists (one-celled organisms and algae), fungi (mushrooms, molds, and other plantlike organisms that do not make their own food), plants, and animals.

The members of a **phylum** have a similar basic structure, but they live in many different places and may be quite different in size and behavior. Different **classes** in a phylum have adapted to different ways of life. Consider that frogs and salamanders (class Amphibia) are adapted to life both in and out of water, and birds (class Aves) are adapted to flying, but both classes belong to the same phylum, Chordata.

Members of a particular **order** have more in common with one another than with those in other orders of the same class. African and Indian elephants (order Proboscidea) and mice and squirrels (order Rodentia) all belong to the class Mammalia. Members of a **family** have even more features in common. Squirrels and chipmunks belong to the family Sciuridae, and mice and rats to the family Muridae.

This tiglon is a cross between a tiger and a lion. Offspring of different species are sterile.

A **genus** is made up of groups that are very similar and have a recent ancestor in common. Members of different species (the groups within a genus) do not usually breed with each other. The genus of bluebirds (*Sialia*) includes the eastern bluebird (*Sialia sialis*), the western bluebird (*Sialia mexicana*), and the mountain bluebird (*Sialia currucoides*). They look very similar but normally breed only with members of their own species.

WHERE WE FIT IN

All humans alive today are classified within the species *sapiens* (Latin for "wise"). Together with some extinct ancestors, we are included in the genus *Homo* (Latin for "human"). The family Hominidae also includes even earlier ancestors. All members of this family (called hominids), as well as monkeys, apes, and lemurs, belong to the order Primates. Primates and other orders—such as those that include cats, bats, dolphins, and elephants—make up the class Mammalia. Mammals and other classes of organisms that have backbones, including amphibians, birds, fish, and reptiles, make up the phylum Chordata. Animals with backbones, together with animals without backbones, make up the kingdom Animalia. So we belong to all seven of these groups: Animalia, Chordata, Mammalia, Primates, Hominidae, *Homo sapiens*.

THE NUMBERS OF DIFFERENT SPECIES IN THE ANIMAL KINGDOM INCLUDE:

about 1,000,000 insects; 30,000 fish; 3,000 amphibians; 6,000 reptiles; 9,000 birds; and 4,000 mammals.

2

WHAT IS AN ANIMAL?

Scientists have classified over a million different kinds of animals, but no one knows how many there really are. Each year hundreds of new animals are discovered. Animals may be very different in appearance and are found in various habitats around the world. But they all have some important things in common that make them members of the animal kingdom, Animalia.

WHAT MAKES AN ANIMAL AN ANIMAL?

Animals are made up of many cells that work together to form a single organism. Each animal cell is enclosed in a thin membrane that permits certain chemicals to pass into

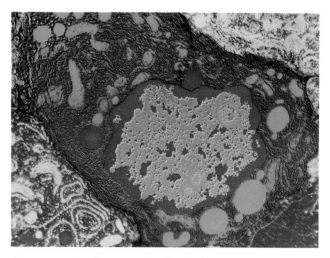

A micrograph of an animal cell. The large pale green structure is the nucleus. An animal cell does not have a rigid cell wall.

and out of it. It does not have a rigid cell wall, as plant cells do.

Animals have complex behaviors. Most can move about, perceive their surroundings with various senses, and learn from experience. Animals are not usually able to make their own food, as plants and some bacteria and one-celled creatures do. In the older, two-kingdom classification system, many single-celled creatures, such as protozoa, were considered one-celled animals.

Animals can be classified according to what they eat. Some, such as cats, dogs, eagles, and spiders, eat other animals. They are called **carnivores**, which comes from Latin words meaning "meat eaters." Animals like cows, deer, sheep, and termites are **herbivores**, "plant eaters." Humans, rats, and pigs are **omnivores** ("everything eaters") and eat both plants and animals. The animal kingdom also includes some scavengers, which feed on dead or decaying matter, and parasites, which live on other animals, sharing their food or even feeding on their body tissues.

Carnivores typically have long, pointed teeth that can tear meat apart. Herbivores have chisel-shaped front teeth to cut off plants and broad, flat back teeth to grind the plant matter. If you look at your own teeth in a mirror, you'll find you have some of each type—perfect equipment for an omnivore.

An eagle (above left) *is a carnivore, a hyena* (above right) *is a scavenger, and a lamprey* (above, attached to fish) *is a parasite.*

WHO'S WHAT AMONG THE ANIMALS

People in the ancient Near East divided animals into five groups: domestic animals, wild animals, creeping animals, flying animals, and water animals. The Greek philosopher Aristotle divided animals into two major groups: those with red blood and those without red blood. He noted whether animals were hairy, feathered, or had shells, and whether they had two or four feet. He further divided the animal kingdom into eleven smaller groups, such as birds, fish, whales, and insects. Aristotle viewed his classification as steps on the "ladder of life," with nonliving things at the bottom, plants on the next rung, and humans at the top of the ladder. This scheme served as the basis of scientific classification for nearly two thousand years, and many of his groupings are still used.

Today the animal kingdom is usually divided into from twenty to thirty-two phyla. One of these is the phylum Chordata, which includes three subphyla: Urochordata (sea squirts), Cephalochordata (lancelets), and Vertebrata (vertebrates). Often, however, the animal kingdom is broken down into just two broad groups: the **vertebrates** and the **invertebrates**.

In this book we'll focus on our closest relatives in the animal kingdom: the vertebrates.

3

THE BACKBONE
IS THE KEY

Picture an animal. What was it? A dog? A cat? A frog? A fish? Chances are, whatever animal you thought of was most likely a vertebrate—a member of the same subphylum to which we humans belong.

BEFORE THE BACKBONE

The phylum Chordata includes the vertebrates, or animals with backbones, along with some not-quite-vertebrates, the lancelets and tunicates. All **chordates** have four important characteristics, at least at some time during their development: (1) a structure called a notochord; (2) a hollow nerve cord running along the animal's back; (3) gill pouches in the inner cavity, or gut; and (4) a tail.

The **notochord** is a stiff rod that runs the length of the animal's body and acts as a support for its skeleton. The fishlike lancelets have a notochord throughout their lives. In the tunicates, only the larval form has a notochord. Among vertebrates it is present only in the embryo and is later replaced by the spine, or vertebral column.

Gill slits, which develop from gill pouches, are openings in the sides of the pharynx (the first portion of the gut). **Tunicates** and **lancelets** use them to filter food. Young fish and amphibians breathe through gill slits and later develop breathing organs called **gills**. Most reptiles, birds, and mammals have gill slits only during their embryonic development.

WHAT MAKES A VERTEBRATE A VERTEBRATE?

In a vertebrate embryo, the nerve cord and notochord are separate at first. But then the notochord develops into the **spine**, which surrounds and protects the nerve cord (the

YOUR COUSIN IS A SEA SQUIRT!

If you were drawing the animals' family tree, where would you put creatures that look like leathery bags and spend their lives attached to the ocean bottom, sucking in seawater and spitting it out? You might conclude that they are primitive invertebrates, like hydras or sea anemones. Actually, they are more closely related to you! A young sea squirt, or tunicate, is a small fishlike larva that swims actively. Its notochord and nerve cord disappear when it turns into an adult. But it still has gill slits, through which the seawater flows.

A colony of tunicates attached to a sponge

INNER SKELETONS

A vertebrate's bony skeleton supports its body, and flexible joints connecting the bones allow it to move easily. Without its inner skeleton, a vertebrate's body would lose its shape. The skeleton provides support without adding too much weight. Buildings, machines, and other things built by people use the same basic principle. What do the inner frameworks of a house, a tent, a car, a kite, and an umbrella look like? How are they similar to a vertebrate's skeleton? In what ways do they differ?

A framework supports a building much in the same way that a skeleton supports a vertebrate's body.

spinal cord). The spine is not a stiff, solid tube. It is made of a series of parts, the vertebrae, linked together like beads in a necklace. The holes in the center of each vertebra form a channel through which the **spinal cord** passes.

In addition to their typical chordate characteristics, vertebrates have some other things in common. They have a definite "head end," where various control centers (the brain) and senses are concentrated. (The spinal cord links the brain with the rest of the body, making it possible to coordinate complicated forms of behavior.) Vertebrates also have **bilateral symmetry**—that is, the parts of the body on each side of the vertebral column are mirror images of each other. And they have a "tube-in-tube" body plan, taking in food at the head end, processing it in the organs of the inner tube (the digestive system or gut), and eliminating waste materials at the other end (the anus).

Among the land vertebrates, the head is usually connected to the body by a narrower neck. The body, or trunk, may be divided into a chest, or thorax, and an abdomen. Some vertebrates have one or two pairs of limbs. All vertebrates have a tail that extends past the anus. But in some, such as humans, the tail is present only during embryonic development. (Actually, you didn't really lose your vertebrate tail. Your trunk

One of the characteristics of vertebrates is that they have bilateral symmetry. One side of this gecko is the mirror image of the other side.

grew faster than your tail, and by the time you were born, the rest of your body had grown past the end of your tail.)

CLASSES, COME TO ORDER!

Although there are more than 40,000 species of vertebrates in the world today, these make up only a small percentage of the total number of animals. The living vertebrate species are divided into eight classes:

hagfish (Myxini)
lampreys (Cephalaspidomorphi)
sharks and other cartilaginous fish (Chondrichthyes)
bony fish (Osteichthyes)
amphibians (Amphibia)
reptiles (Reptilia)
birds (Aves)
mammals (Mammalia)

WHAT A DIFFERENCE A BACKBONE MAKES!

When you eat fish, you have to watch out for the sharp bones. There are a lot of them, buried inside the fish's flesh. Some bones, with holes through their centers, form a kind of flexible rod down the fish's back. This is the spine, or vertebral column, which gives our subphylum its name. The fish's inner bony skeleton provides support for its muscles and helps it to move. A clam or oyster's soft body is supported and protected by two hard outer shells. It has no backbone (nor any other bones)—and so it is an invertebrate.

4

RULERS OF
THE WATER

Fish were the first vertebrates. In some ways they are also the most successful. Four of the eight classes of living vertebrates are fish, and the 30,000 species of fish make up more than half of all the vertebrate species.

WHO NEEDS A JAW?

The earliest vertebrate fossils that scientists have found are jawless fish called **ostracoderms**, which lived about 500 million years ago. These fish measured about a foot (30 centimeters) and lived in the muddy sea bottoms. Their circular mouths were always open, sucking up sediments to filter through their gill slits. Thick bony plates covered their bodies.

The Pacific hagfish (Eptatretus stouti) *is a primitive jawless fish that has survived to this day.*

Taxonomists used to group the primitive fish into one large class, **Agnatha**, which literally means "jawless." Today only the hagfish and lampreys remain, and each has been given its own class. These naked, eel-like fish have skeletons of rubbery cartilage and are very flexible—a hagfish can tie itself in a knot!

RUBBER FISH

The cartilage fish, **Chondrichthyes**, take their class name from the fact that their skeletons are made of cartilage, not bone. There are at least 620 species of cartilaginous fish, including sharks, rays, and dogfish. The largest, the whale sharks (*Rhincodon typus*), grow about 60 feet (18 meters) long and weigh up to 20 tons, and the manta ray has a "wingspan" of 20 feet (6 meters). Ironically, these large creatures are the least ferocious, feeding on plankton and other small marine animals.

ALL THOSE BONES

Most of the fish in the world today—from brightly colored tropical fish to minnows, trout, and tuna—are members of the class **Osteichthyes** (meaning "bony fishes"). Scientists call the period between 345 and 405 million years ago the Age of Fishes because bony fish dominated the earth's lakes and oceans.

As their name suggests, bony fish have skeletons made of bone, not cartilage. Bony fish do not need heavy skeletons for support because water is much denser than air and provides an upward support called buoyancy. You can see how loosely the skeleton is connected when you eat salmon or trout.

In addition to gills, early bony fish also developed lungs for coming to the surface to breathe when there wasn't enough oxygen in the lakes and ponds where they lived. At that time bony fish split into two groups: **lobe-finned fish** and **ray-finned fish**. Lobe-finned fish were the ancestors of amphibians. They used their lungs and gills to breathe. The lungs of ray-finned fish evolved differently. They became **swim bladders**, air sacs that could be filled and deflated to help the fish to float. Most fish living today are ray-finned fish.

JAWS

The great white shark in *Jaws* is one of the scariest "monsters" in movies. But this ferocious predator can hardly compare to its ancient ancestors, the placoderms. These armored fish lived about 400 million years ago. They were the first fish with real, hinged jaws, allowing them to bite off pieces of food. They had also developed fins, which provided more control in swimming. The placoderms are extinct now, but some of their descendants gave rise to the major classes of fish living today, the cartilaginous fish and the bony fish.

There are more than 250 species of sharks, and most are not dangerous to people. White sharks are the largest and most ferocious, growing to more than 20 feet (6 meters) long. Scientists classify the great white shark as kingdom Animalia, phylum Chordata, subphylum Vertebrata, class Chondrichthyes, order Selachii, family Lamnidae, genus *Carcharodon*, species *carcharias*.

Great white shark

THE ULTIMATE FISH

Nearly every kind of fish you've ever heard of—95 percent of all species of fish living today—belong to the order **Teleostei** ("complete bones"). The family Salmonidae includes the Atlantic salmon and many freshwater trout. They are born in rivers, spend most of their lives in the ocean, and then migrate back to their birthplace to spawn (lay their eggs). The family Heterosomata includes many of the fish that we eat, such as halibut, flounder, and sole. These fish are very flat, and both eyes are on the same side of the head. Sea horses (family Syngnathidae, genus *Hippocampus*) are even more unusual. They are covered with bony plates and look like the knights on a chessboard.

THE FISH THAT WALKS

The walking catfish resembles lobe-fin ancestors in its ability to walk on land. When it was imported into Florida, some escaped into local waters, and they have spread across southern Florida by walking from pond to pond!

In the sea horse species, the female lays eggs in a male's pouch. The male carries the eggs until they mature, then releases tiny, live young.

5

A DOUBLE LIFE

Amphibian literally means "leading a double life"—a very appropriate name for this group of animals. Most members of the class **Amphibia** spend part of their lives in the water and part on land.

Amphibians evolved from lunged fish around 350 million years ago. Early amphibians had fishlike bodies with short, stubby legs. They ruled the land for about 100 million years. Most amphibians died off around 200 million years ago. Today this class is represented by about 3,000 species of frogs, toads, newts, salamanders, and rare wormlike apodes. Recently, scientists have noticed that some amphibian species seem to be disappearing. Pollution and other changes humans have made in the environment may be to blame.

AMAZING CHANGES

A human baby looks basically like a miniature adult. Although there are some differences in proportion, a growing child keeps the same set of body parts. But most amphibians pass through a rather startling series of changes as they grow. This sequence of changes is called **metamorphosis** (a "change in shape").

Amphibian eggs are usually laid in the water. Salamanders and frogs lay their eggs in masses; toads lay theirs in long strings. The eggs hatch into young that are called tadpoles. They look like tiny fish with long tails, and they even breathe through gills as fish do. But gradually the tadpoles change. They grow legs and lose their tails (except for the salamanders). Adult amphibians breathe through lungs instead of gills and also take in some oxygen through their moist skin. Amphibians lay eggs with a jellylike coating that must stay moist. These are the reasons why amphibians remain near water.

An amphibian has a three-chambered heart, which is more advanced than a fish's

Frogs lay their eggs in a jellylike mass (left), and toads lay theirs in long strings (right).

two-chambered heart. But, like a fish, an amphibian is cold-blooded. (This doesn't mean that an amphibian is always cold, but that its body temperature changes as the temperature of its environment changes. A frog sunning itself on a rock gets quite warm.)

A TALE OF TAILS

Salamanders and newts belong to the order **Urodela**, which means "visible tail." (Some scientists call the order Caudata, which means "tailed.") There are about 225 species of these lizardlike creatures. Most have four legs, although some have none. Salamanders look most like the early amphibians.

NO TAILS TO TELL

Frogs belong to the order **Anura**, which means "no tail." However, early frogs did have tails. Their body shape changed when jumping to escape from enemies became part of their behavior. Today there are more than 2,500 species of frogs and toads. Both males and females have vocal organs for making sounds, but usually the voice is fully developed only in males. The scientific name for the deep-voiced bullfrogs is *Rana catesbiana*; spring peepers belong to the species *Rana pipiens. Rana temporaria* is another common frog species.

When conditions are dry, certain frogs, like this Pyxicephalus flarigula, *will stay buried for a long time until it rains.*

Toads usually have more compact bodies and shorter hind legs than frogs. A toad has rough skin with bumps. The bumps contain the openings of poison glands that help protect it from being eaten. Toads can stay in dry places much longer than their relatives. More than 100 toad species belong to the genus *Bufo.*

6

THE CREEPY CLASS

The first reptiles evolved nearly 300 million years ago, during a period when many of the lakes and ponds dried up. Some amphibians successfully laid their eggs on land, and, scientists believe, these eventually evolved into reptiles with bodies that were better suited to land life. The early reptiles were called **cotylosaurs**. Like today's crocodiles, cotylosaurs' legs were not long and strong enough to lift their bodies off the ground, so they dragged their bellies and tails when they walked. (The name of the class **Reptilia** means "the creepers.")

As long ages went by, the early reptiles changed into new forms. Their legs became longer and more suited to walking. Smooth amphibian skin evolved into dry, scaly skin. Reptiles' lungs became more efficient, and the crocodilians developed more efficient four-chambered hearts and larger brains.

Reptiles became free of the water because of the "invention" of a new type of egg. In addition to its thick, leathery protective shell, the reptile egg contains its own supply of water and nutrients. So it can be laid on dry land, and the embryo can develop safely inside. (Some reptiles' eggs remain inside the mother's body until they hatch, and the young are born alive.) A young reptile looks like a smaller version of its parents, and it is ready to make it on its own at birth. (A newly hatched poisonous snake can bite right after hatching.)

WHEN DINOSAURS ROAMED THE EARTH

Cotylosaurs gave rise to many types of reptiles, including a variety of dinosaurs. Some 225 million years ago, reptiles existed in great numbers and were split into many different groups. Dinosaurs ruled the land, water, and skies for more than 100 million years, which is why the Mesozoic era (approximately 245 million to 65 million years ago) is called the Age of Reptiles. During this period many reptiles were huge. The largest dinosaur fossil discovered belonged to a dinosaur that was 100–130 feet (30–40 meters) long and weighed 70–95 tons. Some dinosaurs would be tall enough to look over a three-story building.

This is a skeleton of Diplodocus, *a huge plant-eating dinosaur.* Diplodocus *grew to about 90 feet (27 meters) long.*

MOVE OVER T. REX

In 1995, scientists reported that the fossil remains of a huge dinosaur that roamed South America some 100 million years ago had been found in Argentina. This meat-eating monster, named *Giganotosaurus carolinii*, was up to 43 feet (13 meters) long and weighed 6 to 8 tons—almost twice the weight of the ferocious *Tyrannosaurus rex* that lived in North America some 30 million years later.

If you are interested in fossils, keep looking—the bones of *Giganotosaurus* were found by an auto mechanic while searching for fossils in his spare time!

WHERE HAVE ALL THE DINOSAURS GONE?

About 65 million years ago, nearly three-fourths of all living species on earth died out, including all the dinosaurs. Scientists are not sure why. Some believe that a large meteorite struck the earth and sent up a cloud of dust and smoke that blocked the sunlight and polluted the air. As a result, much plant life, which provided food for many dinosaurs, died off. Others think that the dinosaurs had too much competition from mammals who ate their eggs, or that they couldn't adjust to changes in the global climate.

Today there are about 6,000 species of reptiles, which live mostly in tropical areas. Modern reptiles are divided into four orders: snakes and lizards, turtles and tortoises, alligators and crocodiles, and tuataras (a rare reptile from New Zealand).

The longest modern reptile was a 32-foot (10-meter) python. Several kinds of crocodiles grow to 20 feet (6 meters). The Komodo dragons of Indonesia are lizards that can weigh up to 255 pounds (115 kilograms) and grow to 10 feet (3 meters) long. The leatherback sea turtle grows to 6.5 feet (2 meters) long and weighs half a ton.

Above left to right: *Eastern garter snake* (Thamnophis sirtalis); *eastern box turtle* (Terrapene carolina); *tuatara* (Sphenodon punctatus). Left: *American alligator* (Alligator mississippiensis)

BELLY CRAWLERS

Snakes and lizards belong to the order **Squamata** ("scaly"). They came from a common ancestor that lived about 160 million years ago.

Snakes are in a suborder called **Ophidia** (also called Serpentes). There are 2,800 species of snakes, and most are meat eaters. Their long, tubelike, legless bodies with ultraflexible backbones are perfectly designed to slip into narrow holes that lead to animal burrows. A snake's lower jaw can become unhinged to swallow prey that is much bigger than itself. Some snakes kill prey by squeezing it. A few snakes use a venom or poison to kill prey.

About 3,000 species of lizards belong to the suborder **Lacertilia**. Most lizards have long tails and four limbs, but some have no limbs. Males are often more brightly colored than females. Some chameleons can change their coloring to match the surroundings.

MOBILE HOMES

You may have seen a turtle hide inside its shell, but you'll never see a turtle crawl out of its portable home—a turtle shell is attached to the turtle's skeleton! The order **Chelonia** includes 250 species of turtles and tortoises. Turtles live in the oceans, terrapins are freshwater turtles, and tortoises are turtles that live on land. A turtle shell is made of bony plates fused together, covered with a horny layer. Turtles don't have teeth but have a horny beak instead. Sea turtles are mostly meat eaters, while land turtles are mostly vegetarian. Small land turtles, such as the painted turtle (*Chrysemys*), are easily tamed and have been kept as pets.

THE SECRET'S IN THE SNOUT

Twenty-five living species of alligators, crocodiles, caimans, and gavials belong to the order **Crocodylia**. The crocodilians that lived 200 million years ago looked very much like those alive today. Most modern crocodilians live in tropical or subtropical marshes and lakes and are adapted to spending their time both in the water and out of it. So they have an amphibious lifestyle, although they are not amphibians.

Do alligators and crocodiles deserve their scary reputation? Yes, they do—especially the crocodiles! (They are much more aggressive than alligators.) The simplest way to tell a crocodile (family Crocodylidae) from an alligator (family Alligatoridae) is to look at their snout. A crocodile has a pointed snout, and an alligator has a broad snout.

> ### DID YOU KNOW?
> -
> The "horned toads" of the American West are actually lizards (genus *Phrynosoma*), not amphibians.

7

LIFE IN THE AIR

There are more species of birds than of any other vertebrates except for fish. Altogether there are about 9,000 living species in the class **Aves**, and scientists have also classified about 14,000 species of extinct birds. Most birds, such as eagles, gulls, owls, pigeons, and songbirds, can fly.

REPTILE "ROOTS"

The first flying vertebrates were the pterosaurs, huge leathery-winged reptiles. But pterosaurs did not develop into birds; they died out when the dinosaurs did. Scientists believe that small lizardlike **thecodonts** evolved into the earliest birds, such as *Archaeopteryx*. This crow-sized bird lived in forests of central Europe 150 million years ago. It had scaly skin, a long jointed tail, sharp teeth, and curving claws like a reptile, but it had feathered forelimbs like a bird. A 225-million-year-old fossil discovered in Texas, called *Protoavis*, was an even earlier ancestor.

TO BE A BIRD

Modern birds have scales on their legs, a reminder that they evolved from reptiles. But most are well adapted for flying. Reptilian scales on the forelimbs evolved into feathers, and these limbs developed into wings.

Flying uses up a lot of energy. To meet this energy need, birds had to develop a fast rate of metabolism. By maintaining a high internal body temperature, no matter what the external temperature is, the warm-blooded birds can be active at any time of day during any time of year. (Reptiles and insects become inactive when it is cold.) A bird's downy feathers help keep body heat in.

A bird is lighter than other animals of the same size because some of its bones are hollow, and there are air spaces in its body, too. A bird's feathers may weigh more than all the bones of its skeleton!

Birds lay eggs that are protected by hard shells; one or both parents keep them warm with their own bodies while the chicks develop. Young chicks require a long period of parental care, but many kinds of behavior, such as flying and migrating, are not learned—a bird already knows how to do them.

The ostrich egg is the largest bird egg. Compare it with a chicken egg (middle) and a hummingbird egg (bottom).

NOTABLE BIRDS—WINNERS ALL

There are twenty-eight orders of birds. The ostrich (*Struthio camelus*) is the largest living bird, up to 8 feet (2.4 meters) tall and weighing up to 300 pounds (136 kilograms). It is too heavy to fly! California condors (*Gymnogyps californianus*) have a wingspan of more than 10 feet (3 meters). The smallest bird is the bee hummingbird (*Mellisuga helenae*), which is less than 2.5 inches (6.4 centimeters) long and weighs 0.1 ounce (about 3 grams). There are about 100,000 of these hummingbirds in the world, and together they weigh only as much as a single pair of ostriches!

The ostrich (left) is the largest living bird, and the bee hummingbird (right) is the smallest.

The largest bird order is **Passeriformes**, which contains fifty-seven families. This order includes finches, starlings, thrushes, and swallows.

Penguins are the most aquatic birds. There are eighteen living species of penguins, whose bodies are covered with a scalelike wet suit. The fact that developing penguin embryos have feather quills shows that the ancestors of penguins once had typical feathers. Their wings changed into flippers, adapted for swimming.

Scientists believe that ostriches (from Africa); rheas (from South America); emus (from Australia); and kiwis (from New Zealand), which are the flightless **ratite birds**, come from a different evolutionary line from all other birds. They became separated from one another when the continents drifted apart.

BIRD WHO'S WHO

Traditionally, birds are classified by comparing their anatomy and behavior. But newer methods, such as analyzing the proteins in the whites of their eggs, have helped to clear up confusion. Flamingos, in the family Phoenicopteridae, for example, appear to be similar to storks (family Ciconiidae, order **Ciconiiformes**), but studies of their behavior and feather lice suggested that they were related to ducks and geese (family Anatidae, order **Anseriformes**). When scientists analyzed the egg-white proteins, they found that flamingos are most closely related to herons (family Ardeidae in the order Ciconiiformes).

A scientist can look at a bird's beak and tell a lot about its lifestyle. Beaks may be shaped for chiseling, cracking, digging, pecking, piercing, probing, straining, or tearing. Some birds eat seeds. Many eat insects, worms, and other small animals. Woodpeckers (order Piciformes) use their bills like jackhammers to get insects hiding under tree bark. Fish-eating birds include shorebirds and gulls (order **Charadriiformes**), albatrosses (order **Procellariiformes**), and the pelicans (order **Pelecaniformes**) that scoop up their catch in a baglike pouch under the beak. The raptors (birds of prey) have hooked beaks and include two orders: the day-hunting **Falconiformes** (eagles, hawks, and falcons) and the night-hunting **Strigiformes** (owls).

WHY FLY?

Flight gives birds advantages over other vertebrates. They can escape quickly from predators on the ground and can find food more easily. When food is scarce at a certain time of year, they can migrate to another place where food is more abundant. The arc-

The size and shape of a bird's beak tell a lot about how it gets its food. Compare the beak of a woodpecker (left), *a pelican* (center), *and an eagle* (right).

tic tern (*Sterna paradisaea*) spends its summer in the Arctic circle and then flies to the other end of the globe to spend its winter in Antarctica—that's about 25,000 miles (40,000 kilometers) traveled each year!

BIRD-WATCHING

Birding is a popular hobby. Spotting a species you've never seen before can be a real thrill. What characteristics would you watch for, to identify the birds you see? Field guides, with descriptions and pictures, aid bird-watchers in identifying the birds they observe. Such guides may group the birds according to their scientific classifications, or they may be organized according to other characteristics, such as location, size, and color. Tapes of birdsongs can also be helpful, since each species sings its own characteristic songs.

8

OUR OWN CLASS

The most highly developed animals belong to the class **Mammalia**. Mammals are warm-blooded vertebrates whose females nurse their young with milk. Most mammals have a coat of hair (long thin strands made mostly of a protein called keratin) that acts as insulation to keep body heat from escaping. All mammals have hair at some stage in their development—even those, such as whales and dolphins, that are hairless as adults. (Their heat-retaining insulation is a layer of fatty blubber under the skin.)

Most mammals are **placental mammals**, belonging to subclass **Eutheria**. The young of these mammals develop inside the mother's body, receiving nourishment through a structure called the placenta.

Mammals' brains, in proportion to body size, are larger than those of any other animals. Mammals have four-chambered hearts and breathe with lungs. A dome-shaped sheet of muscle called the diaphragm aids in breathing and divides the body into two cavities: the chest and the abdomen.

Most mammals live on land. However, bats fly, and whales, dolphins, seals, and manatees live in water.

The blue whale is the largest animal that ever lived; it can grow to more than 100 feet (30 meters) long and can weigh 150 tons. Water helps to hold up whales' huge bulk. Land animals cannot grow as large. The elephant is the largest land animal alive today. It can weigh up to 20 tons. The smallest mammal is the Kitti's hog-nosed bat of Thailand, which is the size of a bumblebee and weighs only 0.07 ounce (2 grams).

THE RISE OF MAMMALS

Mammals arose before dinosaurs ruled the earth. Early mammals evolved from reptiles. The **therapsids** were fierce, heavyset, mammal-like reptiles that lived between 225 and

This model of the blue whale is 92 feet (28 meters) long.

180 million years ago. By around 200 million years ago, rat-sized shrewlike mammals had evolved. But it wasn't until 65 million years ago, after the dinosaurs disappeared, that mammals began to spread widely and dominate the earth.

Today there are about 4,500 living mammal species. That may not seem like much compared to one million insect species. But the current geological era (Cenozoic) is called the Age of Mammals because mammals have spread throughout the world. Based on their anatomy and behavior, scientists have divided mammals into nineteen orders (the number of species given is approximate in most cases):

Monotremata: Egg-laying mammals (3 species: echidnas, duck-billed platypuses)

Marsupialia: Pouched mammals (260 species: kangaroos, koalas, opossums, etc.)

Insectivora: "Insect eaters" (380 species: moles, shrews, hedgehogs)

Dermoptera: Flying lemurs (colugos) (2 species)

Chiroptera: Bats (900 species)

Primates: Monkeys, lemurs, apes, and humans (180 species)

Edentata: Anteaters, armadillos, and sloths (30 species)

Pholidota:	Pangolins (7 species)
Lagomorpha:	Hares, pikas, and rabbits (65 species)
Rodentia:	Rodents (1,750 species, including beavers, gophers, mice, rats, porcupines, and squirrels)
Cetacea:	Dolphins, porpoises, and whales (80 species)
Carnivora:	Carnivores ("meat eaters") (270 species, including bears, cats, raccoons, weasels, and wolves)
Pinnipedia:	"Fin feet" (34 species of seals, sea lions, and walruses; sometimes classified as carnivores)
Tubulidentata:	Aardvark (1 species)
Proboscidea:	Elephants (2 species: African and Indian)
Hyracoidea:	Hyraxes (7 species)
Sirenia:	"Sea cows" (4 species of dugongs and manatees)
Perissodactyla:	Odd-toed ungulates (17 species, including horses, rhinoceroses, and tapirs)
Artiodactyla:	Even-toed ungulates (185 species, including antelopes, bison, camels, cattle, deer, giraffes, goats, hippopotamuses, hogs, and sheep)

MAMMALS VERSUS REPTILES

A land mammal's skeleton is more efficiently engineered for moving about on land than a reptile's. When a mammal walks, it lifts its body off the ground; amphibians and reptiles are built closer to the ground, and their tracks typically show not only footprints but marks made by dragging their bellies and tails. A mammal's brain is larger than a reptile's brain, and the cerebrum, or "thinking brain," is more developed. Mammal jaws are built differently from reptile jaws, too. The mammalian lower jaw is a single bone, and the upper jaw is stationary—so, unlike a snake, a mammal cannot eat anything larger than itself. It has to eat smaller food items, or use its teeth to tear up larger ones. Mammals have only two sets of teeth in a lifetime, compared to many in reptiles.

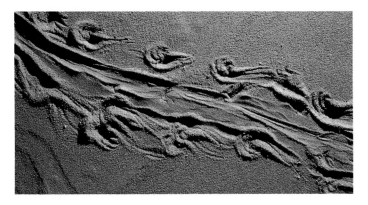

Footed amphibians and reptiles leave a track such as this, showing that they dragged their bellies and tails as they walked along.

BABY MAMMALS

Many mammals are born at a very immature stage, before they have finished developing. The newborn young of many rodents and of carnivores such as bears and foxes are completely helpless: their eyes are closed, they can't hear, and they can barely move. But newborn horses and sheep can walk within a few minutes, and within an hour can run with their mothers!

These ten-day-old bear cubs still have their eyes and ears closed.

TAMING WILD MAMMALS

People began domesticating, or taming, wild mammals about 10,000 years ago. Dogs were among the first domesticated species. Later the wild ancestors of cattle, goats, hogs, and sheep were domesticated as sources of meat. Some also provided milk, and their hair and skins were used to make clothing. Buffaloes, camels, elephants, goats, horses, llamas, reindeer, oxen, and even dogs have all been used to carry people or other loads. Today cats, dogs, hamsters, and rabbits are popular pets.

DID YOU KNOW?

- - - - - - - - - - - - - - - - - - - -

Armadillos always give birth to identical quadruplets.

9

PRIMITIVE MAMMALS

Researchers believe that the earth's continents were once joined. But about sixty-five million years ago the Australian continent split from the main landmass. The mammals on that isolated continent were caught in a kind of time warp. They missed a major change and retained some important characteristics of the first primitive mammals.

ODDBALL MAMMALS

Scientists in the 1800s were faced with a real puzzle. Most of the animals that had been discovered fit fairly neatly into the classification scheme popularized by Carl Linnaeus. But where would you put an animal like the duck-billed platypus? It has a bill and webbed feet like a duck. It has poison glands and lays leathery eggs like a reptile. It has fur, is warm-blooded, and feeds its young with milk like a mammal (but the mother does not have nipples). Finally the scientists decided that hair and milk were the most important features. So it was assigned to Monotremata, the most primitive order of mammals. This order also includes two species of echidnas, or spiny anteaters, which also have fur, lay eggs, and feed milk to their young. Living monotremes are found only in Australia, New Guinea, and Tasmania.

Duck-billed platypus

POCKETS ARE HANDY

Marsupials' young are born before they are fully developed—some as little as eight days after fertilization! Each tiny baby, about the size of a kidney bean, crawls up the mother's stomach into a pouch (called a marsupium). It clamps its mouth onto one of the mother's mammary nipples and stays in the pouch, safe and protected, for months more until it is ready to come out.

At one time, most of the mammals on earth were marsupials. Fossil evidence suggests that the Australian continent separated from the other landmasses before placental mammals became widespread. So nearly all the native mammals of Australia and the nearby islands are marsupials—about two-thirds of the 260 marsupial species that still remain. The Australian marsupials are a varied group, including herbivores, carnivores, and insectivores; marsupials that live on the ground, in trees, or in underground burrows. In addition to kangaroos, whose large hind legs are adapted for leaping, there are marsupials that resemble mice, cats, wolves, and various other placental mammals.

This species of opossum is the only marsupial in North America today.

In the rest of the world, the only marsupials that survived were opossums. About 80 kinds of opossums (family Didelphidae) live in Central and South America. Marsupials lived in North America 40 to 100 million years ago, but they became extinct. Three to four million years ago, when North and South America became linked, one species of opossum made its way back to North America. This is the only marsupial in Canada and the United States today.

TOOTHLESS, FOR THE MOST PART

South American anteaters are primitive placental mammals that belong to the order Edentata. An anteater has a long, tubular jaw with a tiny slit at the end for the mouth, from which a long sticky tongue whips out to scoop up termites. The aardvark of South Africa (order Tubulidentata) has a similar lifestyle but is not related to the anteater.

The name of the order means "without teeth," but some members, the tree sloths and armadillos, have enamelless teeth at the back of their mouths. Armadillos' bony, platelike "armor" covers their heads, backs, and flanks. When an armadillo is threatened, it curls into a ball to protect its soft belly. Pangolins (order Pholidota) also wear coats of armor—overlapping horny plates that make them look like moving pinecones.

10

RODENTS, RABBITS, AND OTHER SMALL MAMMALS

Beavers, gophers, porcupines, mice, rats, and squirrels are all rodents. But rabbits and hares do not belong to the order Rodentia, although they do have some similar traits and are among the rodents' closest relatives. Both rodents and lagomorphs (rabbits and hares) have teeth and intestines that are adapted to a vegetarian diet. Their chisel-like front teeth are designed for gnawing or scraping seeds and other hard plant matter. In fact, the name Rodentia comes from a word meaning "to gnaw."

UNDERFOOT EVERYWHERE

Rodents are the most numerous of all mammals—40 percent of the mammal species!—and are also found in more areas of the world than other mammals. There are about thirty-three different families of rodents.

Did you know that a rodent's front teeth (incisors) keep growing throughout its life? That's why rats and mice living in a house can be so destructive: they must gnaw on things constantly to wear down their front teeth. Otherwise the incisors would grow so long that the rodent could not close its mouth!

NOTABLE RODENTS

The South American capybara (*Hydrochaerus hydrochaeris*) is the largest rodent—about the size of a small pig. The African pygmy mouse (*Mus minutoides*) is the smallest rodent—about 3 inches long (7.5 centimeters).

Beavers, the largest rodents in North America, have adapted to life in the water and have developed webbed feet and waterproof fur. They gnaw tree trunks and branches to build dams on rivers and streams, forming ponds.

The North American beaver is Castor canadensis. *At one time, they were very important to the fur-trapping trade in Canada and the United States. A beaver keeps growing for its entire life and can weigh from 40 to 95 pounds (18 to 43 kilograms).*

Black rats (*Rattus rattus*) and Norway rats (*Rattus norvegicus*) were originally found in Asian forests. Humans accidentally took them all around the world when rats stowed away on ships. Rats and other rodents sometimes spread diseases—for example, plague, which is carried by fleas that may live in rodent fur.

LEAPING LAGOMORPHS

Rabbits, hares, and pikas look like rodents, but they have two pairs of upper incisors, compared to only one pair in a rodent's upper jaw. The name of their order, Lagomorpha, means "hare-shaped."

How do you tell the difference between a hare and a rabbit? Hares have longer hind legs and longer ears than rabbits. (A hare's ears are longer than its head.) Hares are born with fur, but rabbits are born naked. Pikas belong to the same order but don't look very hare-shaped: they have small ears and almost no tail, and all four legs are the same length.

Rabbits and hares belong to order Lagomorpha. People often confuse hares and rabbits, but a rabbit, such as the Eastern cottontail (left), has shorter ears than a hare (right).

Did you know that the jackrabbit (*Lepus californicus*) is really a hare? Its huge ears give it away. The cottontail rabbits (genus *Sylvilagus*) of North America may look very much like the rabbits sold in pet stores, but they are really more closely related to hares. The breeds of pet rabbits all belong to the species *Oryctolagus cuniculus* and originally came from Europe.

BUG EATERS

Shrews, moles, and hedgehogs look like rodents, but they are more primitive. They are found all around the world except in Australasia and polar regions. The name of their order, Insectivora, means "insect eaters."

Shrews are among the smallest mammals—the North American pygmy shrew is 3.5 inches (9 centimeters) long and weighs less than a penny. Shrews are constantly hungry and often eat enough insects, worms, and other prey at a single meal to equal their whole body weight.

Moles burrow in the ground, loosening soil with short, strong forelimbs. A mole's eyes are tiny and weak; in its underground life, it depends more on its sense of smell and the sensitive "feelers" at the tip of its snout.

Hedgehogs are larger than shrews and moles, and are native only to the Old World. Hedgehogs have a coat of spines to protect them. The American porcupines (in the rodent order) also have a coat of spines (quills), but they are not closely related to hedgehogs.

MAMMALS THAT FLY

The German word for bat literally means "flying mouse," and the small bats actually do look rather like rats or mice with wings. Some of the largest bats look more like foxes. Altogether, bats account for one quarter of all mammal species!

Bats are the only mammals that can really fly. (Flying squirrels and flying lemurs can only glide from branch to branch or down to the ground.) Unlike birds, whose whole forearms have been modified into feather-covered wings, bats have wings more like kites or umbrellas. Each wing is formed by a membrane of skin, supported by long, slender finger bones. So the name of the bat order, Chiroptera, which literally means "hand-wing," is quite appropriate.

The little brown bat (Myotis lucifugus) *has a wingspan of approximately 8 inches (20 centimeters). About forty species of bats, including this one, live in Canada and the United States.*

Most bats feed on beetles, moths, and other night-flying insects. A bat uses a sophisticated **echolocation** system to find insects at night. As it flies, it sends out high-pitched squeaks. These sound signals bounce off objects in the bat's path, and its sensitive ears pick up the echoes.

In tropical regions there are many different kinds of bats. Some eat fruit, some eat fish—and vampire bats really do drink blood.

FACT FROM FICTION

The winged monkeys that captured Dorothy and her friends in *The Wizard of Oz* were somewhat similar to giant flying foxes, the largest fruit bats. Recently taxonomists have found evidence that these bats are actually close relatives of the primates, the order to which monkeys belong.

11

THE HUNTERS

Land animals that eat flesh are placed in the order Carnivora. This includes cats, hyenas, dogs, weasels, bears, and raccoons. Most carnivores prey on other animals, but some, such as hyenas, usually eat dead animals. Bears eat many foods, including leaves and berries; foxes also have a varied diet. Pandas are classified among the carnivores (in the same family as raccoons), but they are not meat eaters. Pandas eat mostly bamboo shoots and are an endangered species today because the shoots they eat are getting scarcer.

Many carnivores have fur that is very soft and attractive. People have hunted some of them to near extinction for their pelts. Others, such as mink and sable, are raised on fur farms.

Carnivores were among the first mammals. Primitive carnivores, which lived before the dinosaurs disappeared, were replaced by two main groups: cat- and doglike ancestors, from which all of the modern carnivores descended. Carnivores are native to all parts of the world except for Australia, New Zealand, and islands in the Pacific. (Dingoes, the "wild" dogs of Australia, are descendants of domesticated dogs that accompanied the first human settlers thousands of years ago.)

WELL-DESIGNED HUNTERS

Most carnivores are well adapted to a hunting life, with large canine teeth for holding and tearing prey. Their blood contains a special kind of "good cholesterol" that allows them to eat a high-fat meat diet without getting heart attacks. Many carnivores are very fast. The cheetah, a member of the cat family, is the fastest land animal on the earth. In the dog family, wolves and the wild dogs of Africa are tireless long-distance runners.

Carnivores usually have very good eyesight, a great sense of smell, and sharp hearing, too. Most are fairly intelligent.

Lions live and hunt in small groups called prides, consisting of males, females, and young. Members of the dog family usually hunt in larger packs. Other carnivores are not as social, but even the "loners" form close-knit family units while raising their young. Mothers—and sometimes fathers, too—care for the young for a long time.

This Alaskan brown bear shows the sharp teeth and claws typical of a carnivore. Bears that live near populated areas may be attracted by garbage, and accidental meetings with humans can have tragic results.

POINTS OF INTEREST

Members of the weasel family are found in many of the colder parts of the world. Otters are found in the water and martens in trees. The slim-bodied weasels and ferrets can wriggle into their prey's burrows to hunt.

The banded mongoose of India is famous for preying on poisonous snakes.

Many cats can climb trees. Jaguars and tigers can also swim. Most cats live alone. Leopards are found in tropical rain forests of Africa and Asia.

Raccoons live near humans and feed on almost anything. They can climb and swim well. With their characteristic "bandit" mask and their clever ways, raccoons may be appealing. Recently, though, they have become a health problem, spreading rabies to rural and suburban areas.

WHERE DO THEY FIT IN?

Foxes look rather doglike, but they don't live in packs. And their hunting style—sneaking up on their prey and pouncing—is more like that of cats. Taxonomists have placed them in the dog family, Canidae.

Hyenas look rather doglike, too, but there are so many differences that taxonomists have classified them in a separate family, Hyaenidae.

Jackals are definitely dogs, though. In fact, they can breed with wolves, coyotes, and even domestic dogs.

Raccoons belong to the same family as pandas, Procyonidae, although at first glance about the only thing they seem to have in common is a mask. Raccoons have a varied diet, which may include your garbage.

12

SEA MAMMALS

Whales, dolphins, and porpoises, in the order Cetacea, can be found in all of the world's oceans. Whales are the largest animals that ever lived, and also among the most intelligent. Even though they live in the water, whales have lungs like us and must come to the surface to breathe through blowholes at the tops of their heads. When a whale dives underwater, this blowhole is tightly closed so that water doesn't get into its lungs.

OCEAN GIANTS

Cetaceans and carnivores are descended from a common ancestor that lived 65 million years ago. Whales left the land and evolved to become completely adapted to living in the water. Front limbs became steering paddles, hind limbs disappeared, and whales developed tail flukes to help them move.

A southern right whale is a baleen whale, which feeds by straining plankton through hundreds of thin plates in its mouth. The plates are made of the same material as human fingernails.

There are two groups of whales. Baleen whales range from 20 to 100 feet (6 to 30 meters) long. Toothed whales are mostly smaller but include many more species.

Baleen whales have "whalebones" instead of teeth. These are triangular plates of horny material, called **baleen**, in the roof of the mouth, which strain out tiny shrimplike water creatures called krill. This is all baleen whales eat. Most toothed whales have many teeth and eat fish and squids. Dolphins and porpoises also have teeth and hunt sea animals.

Whales can grow to such huge sizes because their bodies are supported by the water. The blue whale (*Sibbaldus musculus*) is the largest living animal. One female was nearly 113 feet (34 meters) long.

Scientists believe that whales communicate with one another by a complicated system of sounds, which may be like a form of language. Some dolphins have been taught to recognize and imitate sounds of human speech. Both whales and dolphins use echolocation as a sonar system in much the same way as bats do—to find prey and to orient themselves.

This blue whale skeleton gives an idea of the size of this huge creature.

Many whales are endangered by human activities. Throughout history people have hunted whales for food and for their blubber and other parts, which have been used in various industries. The sperm whale (*Physeter catodon*), blue whale (*Sibbaldus musculus*), humpback whale (*Megaptera novaeangliae*), and fin whale (*Balaenoptera physalus*) are whales that have been dangerously overhunted.

NOTABLE CETACEANS

The male narwhal (*Monodon monoceros*), found in Arctic seas, has a nearly 10-foot (3-meter) pointed tusk that develops from one of its teeth. Narwhal tusks are thought to be the origin of the unicorn myths.

Killer whales, or orcas (*Orcinus orca*), are the most ferocious of the whales. These black-and-white whales will prey on practically anything that swims.

The bottle-nosed dolphin (*Tursiops truncatus*) is the most familiar member of the whale order. These dolphins grow to a length of 10 feet (3 meters) and are very intelligent.

FLIPPER FEET

Seals, sea lions, and walruses adapted to life mostly in water, and are usually placed in their own order, Pinnipedia ("fin feet"). (Some taxonomists place them with the carnivores.) Like whales and dolphins, seals evolved a streamlined shape. They have a thick layer of blubber under their skin, but their bodies are covered with a coat of sleek fur. Seal limbs are modified into flippers, which are effective for swimming but make seals rather clumsy when they come out on land.

The walrus is the only member of its family. This relative of the seal eats mollusks that it "rakes up" from the ocean bottom with its tusks (long upper canine teeth). The tusks of a male walrus may be more than 3 feet (1 meter) long!

A group of walruses (Odobenus rosmarus)

NOT EXACTLY MERMAIDS

The "sea cows" include four species of dugongs and manatees. These strange-looking water-dwelling mammals have flattened muzzles, paddlelike forelimbs, and no hind legs—not very much like the alluring mythical sirens for which their order, Sirenia, was named.

The dugong is a plant-eating sea mammal, and it is an endangered species. An adult usually weighs about 600 pounds (270 kilograms) and can live up to about seventy years.

Like whales, dugongs and manatees have a streamlined shape and a fishlike tail, and they are nearly hairless. (An adult manatee has only a few sparse whiskers, which act as "feelers" that help it to navigate in the muddy shallow waters where it lives.) But the ancestor of the manatees and dugongs that returned to the sea was not the same ancient mammal that produced the whales and dolphins. It was more closely related to elephants.

13

HOOFED MAMMALS

There are more than 200 species of hoofed animals, or **ungulates** (from the Latin word for "hoof"). Ungulates are all herbivores; they feed on vegetation, which they chew with specialized teeth. Many of them have horns or antlers on their foreheads.

Hoofs are really huge toenails. The ancestors of these animals walked on their toes, not on the full length of the foot as humans do. Eventually the toenails evolved to be bigger and bigger, and the original foot became part of the leg. This increased the length of the leg, allowing ungulates to run faster in escaping from predators. Meanwhile, some of the five toes in the standard mammalian foot became smaller or disappeared entirely.

Ungulates first arose about 60 million years ago. Gradually two different lines developed. Today taxonomists distinguish them by the number of toes on each foot.

The even-toed ungulates (order Artiodactyla, about 185 species) have feet with two or four toes. When odd-toed ungulates (order Perissodactyla, 17 species) walk or run, all their body weight is borne by their middle toes.

The even-toed group (including cows, pigs, sheep, and goats, as well as deer, antelope, camels, hippopotamuses, and giraffes) and the odd-toed ungulates (the horse group) may seem rather similar, but they have been separate groups for millions of years. Scientists have determined by examining teeth and other clues that elephants, rock hyraxes (which look like hoofed guinea pigs), and sea cows are related to ungulates.

Most ungulates live in large groups called herds. Members of the herd may help one another in caring for the young and in defending the weaker members of the group from predators.

EVEN TOES

Pigs and peccaries (piglike mammals found in South America) are the most primitive even-toed ungulates. They have lost only one toe (corresponding to the "thumb") and thus have four toes on each foot. But the two middle toes are much larger than the outer ones. In deer, antelope, and cattle, the outer toes are even smaller and may not touch the ground. Camels and their South American relatives, llamas, have only two toes on each foot.

Cattle, antelope, deer, goats, and sheep have multiple-compartment stomachs in which food is stored, then regurgitated and rechewed ("chewing the cud"). Bacteria in the stomach compartments help to break down fibers in the plants these herbivores eat.

The even-toed ungulates include nearly all the animals that have been domesticated as sources of meat, as well as species that are raised for their wool and as beasts of burden. A notable wild member of the group is the hippopotamus. Its name means "river horse," and this huge mammal spends most of its time in or near the water. The giraffe is another even-toed ungulate. Although a giraffe's neck may be over 6 feet (nearly 2 meters) long, it has exactly the same number of vertebrae as the necks of mice, humans, and other mammals.

A pig has four toes on each foot, with two center toes that are much larger than the toe on either side. Each toe ends in a hoof.

The giraffe (Giraffa camelopardalis) is an even-toed ungulate. Its hooves are split into two parts, each part consisting of the hardened tip of one toe. The giraffe is the tallest of all land animals.

ODD TOES

There were once more odd-toed ungulates. Today only the horse group (which includes zebras, donkeys, and mules), rhinoceroses, and tapirs remain. None of the odd-toed ungulates chews its cud, or has any real horns. Rhinos' "horns" are really compressed hair. Rhinos have three toes on each foot. Tapirs have four toes on the front feet and three on the hind feet. Horses have only one toe on each foot.

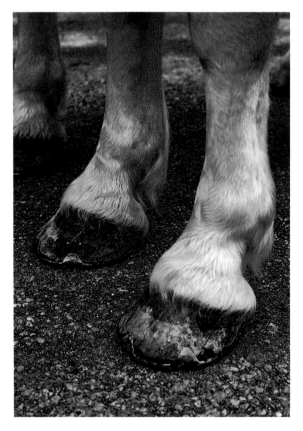

WHAT IS A MULE?

The horse clan (family Equidae) are so closely related that the different species can interbreed. But crossbred offspring of horses (*Equus caballus*) and donkeys (*Equus asinus*) are sterile and cannot have young of their own. The offspring of a mare (female horse) and a jackass (male donkey) is called a mule; that of a stallion (male horse) and a jenny (female donkey) is a hinny.

A horse has only one toe on each foot, ending in a hoof. A horse actually walks on the tips of its toes. Frequently, lightweight metal shoes are nailed painlessly to a horse's hooves to protect them.

HOSE-NOSES

Elephants are the largest living land mammals. The name of their order, Proboscidea, refers to the elephant's trunk, an elongated, flexible tube that is formed from its nose and upper lip and serves as a combination nose, hose, and grasping tool. Elephants' upper incisors developed into huge tusks. They have only four other teeth—huge grinding molars, which gradually wear out, move forward, and are replaced by new pairs of teeth that move in behind them.

Elephantlike mammals originally appeared in Africa and spread to Europe, Asia, and North America. The ancient members of the order included the huge mastodons and mammoths. But today there are only two species of elephants left: the Indian elephant (*Elephas maximus*) of southern Asia and the African elephant (*Loxodonta africana*). African elephants are larger, and they also have larger ears. Another difference is that Indian elephants have four hoofs on each hind foot and African elephants have only three. Both species are very intelligent and can be trained to do tricks or work in the fields and forests.

WHAT DO AN ELEPHANT AND A BALLERINA HAVE IN COMMON?

Both can walk on their toes. But an elephant is too heavy to toe-dance, or even to gallop.

ACTIVITY

Make a list of the animals humans have domesticated. To what taxonomic groups does each belong? Which group contains the largest number of domesticated animals? Do you see any relationships between the classification of domesticated animals and the uses humans make of them?

*The Indian elephant (*Elephas maximus*) is still used today in several countries to carry heavy loads. The elephant population is in danger because of shrinking habitats and poaching.*

14

-- -- -- -- -- -- -- --

US AND LIKE US

-- -- -- -- -- -- -- --

The name of the order Primates comes from a word meaning "first," and for most people Primates is the group of animals first in importance. The reason is that this order includes the mammals most similar to us—our closest relatives—as well as our own species, *Homo sapiens*. Although some primates have highly developed brains, this was actually one of the earliest mammalian groups to evolve. Primates are believed to be the descendants of tree shrews, insectivores that first moved into the trees about 60 million years ago.

The primates living today include two suborders: **Prosimii**, the prosimians (meaning "before monkeys": the lemurs and tarsiers); and **Anthropoidea**, or anthropoids ("humanlike": monkeys, apes, and humans). Except for humans, primates are found mostly in tropical areas, and most live in trees. Primates have a number of traits that made them fit for life in the treetops and aided their further evolution:

- flat-nailed, five-fingered hands with opposable thumbs—good for grasping branches and manipulating objects;
- all four types of teeth: canines, incisors, premolars, and molars, allowing them to eat all kinds of food;
- eyes facing forward, permitting sharp, three-dimensional vision and good depth perception;
- large brains, with a convoluted (wrinkled and ridged) cerebral cortex that increases the brain area even more.

NOT QUITE MONKEYS

Lemurs and tarsiers are small, tree-dwelling, squirrel-like insect eaters, but they are primates because they have opposable thumbs and a sharp sense of sight. Lemurs live

A family of ring-tailed lemurs

only on the island of Madagascar. Tarsiers live in forests in the Philippines, Borneo, and Sumatra.

OUR LITTLE COUSINS

The anthropoids—monkeys, apes, and humans—typically have complex social behavior. Parents care for the young for long periods of time, and individuals live in family units or larger groups. In many species communication skills are highly developed.

There are two groups of monkeys. New World monkeys (superfamily **Ceboidea**) are found in tropical forests in Central and South America and include howler monkeys, capuchins, marmosets, and tamarins. Old World monkeys (superfamily **Cercopithecoidea**) are found in the tropics of Asia and Africa and include the rhesus monkeys from Southeast Asia and northern India used in medical research, and baboons and mandrills of Africa. Baboons live on the ground, but are still good climbers.

The baboon (far left) belongs to the Old World group of monkeys. It has a more pronounced nose than New World monkeys, such as the red howler monkey (Alouatta seniculus), shown at near left.

The easiest way to tell the two types of monkeys apart is by the shape of the nose. New World monkeys have flattish noses with nostrils that are set wide apart. Old World monkeys have more pronounced noses with nostrils close together. Another key difference is that New World monkeys have long tails that are used for grasping, almost like a "fifth hand." Many of the Old World monkeys have short tails or no tail at all.

APES LIKE US

Apes and **hominids** (humans and their direct ancestors) form a group called the **hominoids** (resembling or related to humans). The earliest known hominoids lived in the Old World 20 to 25 million years ago. Apes are larger and have larger brains than monkeys, have no visible tail, and never lived in the New World. Unlike humans, apes have arms that are longer than their legs.

Living apes are classified into two families: the lesser apes (Hylobatidae)—the siamangs and gibbons of Southeast Asia—can leap and swing by their arms at great speeds through the treetops; the great apes (Pongidae) include orangutans, gorillas, and chimpanzees. They are much bigger than the lesser apes and spend most of their time on the ground, except when they sleep.

Orangutans (*Pongo pygmaeus*) live in forests of Sumatra and Borneo. Their name means "man of the woods." They are intelligent and social.

Gorillas (*Gorilla gorilla*) are the biggest and strongest primates, but these giants are mostly vegetarians. They are found in mist forests of western and central Africa. Male gorillas may be nearly 7 feet (2 meters) tall and weigh 450 pounds (200 kilograms). Gorillas spend most of their time on the ground and lean on their knuckles when they walk. Scientists have found that they are very intelligent and can be taught to understand many words and phrases.

This chimpanzee has found that a stick makes a great tool to clean the teeth

Chimpanzees (*Pan troglodytes*) share 99 percent of our genes! They are our closest living relatives. Chimps live in forests of western and central Africa in family groups. They use sticks and grass as tools and can be trained to accomplish difficult tasks, such as learning to communicate in sign language.

HUMAN INTEREST

Early hominids left the trees and moved into open fields. Carnivores were their greatest enemies. Hominids were able to survive mainly because of their intelligence and their opposable thumbs, which allowed them to make tools and weapons. Over time hominids evolved to be less apelike and more like modern humans.

All humans alive today belong to the same species, *Homo sapiens*, which means "wise (or knowing) human." Humans are distinct from other primates because of our upright posture, long legs and shorter arms, small jaw, high forehead, and less body hair. Humans are omnivores—we can eat meat or vegetables and fruits. We can't smell, taste, hear, see, run, swim, or climb better than many other mammals, but our brains are much more developed. We can reason, learn, speak, and have a much greater impact on the fate of the world in which we live.

How will humans evolve in the future? In much of the world, people no longer have to be skilled hunters and gatherers—the food they need is available in markets and grocery stores. Poorer nations can be helped by more developed ones. Will traits for intellectual abilities be important in our future evolution? Or maybe resistance to disease, pollution, and stress will be keys to our survival.

WHICH CAME FIRST: THE HAND, THE FOOT, OR THE BRAIN?

Some scientists speculate that human development took a big leap forward when primitive hominids came down from the trees to live on the plains. The upright posture—standing and walking on two legs—freed the hands to carry and manipulate things, and to make tools. Meanwhile, the "thinking" part of the brain expanded and developed, and the structure of the face and neck changed to permit speech—a way to exchange ideas and pass on knowledge.

IDENTIKEY

Naturalists may use identification keys to help them in identifying plants and animals. Suppose you caught a small, brown-furred animal in a live trap in your house. Here's an "identikey" to help you determine whether it is a mouse, and if so, what kind.

1. You live in a city	**Probably a house mouse**
You live in a suburban or rural area	**Go to step 2**
2. Long, pointed snout; tiny eyes; very active	**Long-tailed shrew**
Mouselike head, large ears and eyes	**Go to step 3**
3. Naked, scaly-looking tail	**House mouse**
Fur on tail	**Go to step 4**
4. Hind legs much longer than forelegs, hairy tail	**White-footed mouse**
Hind legs somewhat longer, little hair on tail	**Harvest mouse**

A LITTLE LATIN HELPS

Knowing some basic Latin and Greek "building blocks" can help you guess the meaning of scientific terms.

a-	without	*gam-*	joined; pertaining to mating	*oo-*	egg
amphi-	both			*oste(o)-*	bone
anthrop(o)-	human	*gen-*	gene, hereditary	*ov(o)-*	egg
arthr(o)-	joint(ed)	*herb(i)-*	plant	*-ped, -pod*	foot, leg
bi-	two	*hetero-*	different	*-phil*	loving
carn(i)-	meat	*hippo-*	horse	*-phor(e)*	carrier
-coel	cavity	*homo-*	same	*poly-*	many
-dactyl	digits, toes, fingers	*hydr-*	water	*pro-*	before
		-ichthy	fish	*prot(o)-*	first
deca-	ten	*in-*	in, not	*-ptera*	wings
-dent, -dont	tooth	*lag(o)-*	hare	*-saur*	reptile
di-	two	*maxi-*	big	*-som(e)*	body
endo-	inside	*mini-*	little	*-sperm*	seed
entomo-	insect	*mon(o)-*	one	*terr(a)-*	land
eu-	true	*-morph*	form	*vir-*	poison
exo-	outside	*oct(a)-*	eight	*-vore*	eating
-form(es)	in the form of, resembling	*-oid*	like	*vulgaris*	common
		omni-	everything	*zo(o)-*	animal

GLOSSARY

Agnatha — jawless fish; in some older classification systems, a class including both lampreys and hagfish as well as extinct ostracoderms.

Amphibia — amphibians; a class of vertebrates that typically spend part of their life in water and part on land; includes frogs, toads, and salamanders.

Anseriformes — an order of birds including ducks, geese, and swans.

Anthropoidea — anthropoids; a primate suborder including monkeys, apes, and humans.

Anura — the order of tailless amphibians, including frogs and toads.

Artiodactyla — even-toed ungulates; a mammalian order including antelopes, bison, camels, cattle, deer, giraffes, goats, hippopotamuses, hogs, and sheep.

Aves — birds; a class of vertebrates with feathers. Most birds can fly.

baleen — "whalebone"; triangular plates of horny material in the roof of the mouth in some whales; used to filter plankton, including small shrimplike krill, out of the water.

bilateral symmetry — a body form with two distinct halves, each of which is an approximate mirror image of the other.

binomial nomenclature — the system of scientific naming devised by Carl Linnaeus, in which each organism is assigned a genus and a species name.

carnivores — a mammalian order (**Carnivora**) of meat eaters including bears, cats, raccoons, weasels, and wolves.

Ceboidea — primate superfamily; includes New World monkeys found in Central and South America.

Cercopithecoidea — a primate superfamily; includes Old World monkeys found in the tropics of Asia and Africa.

Cetacea — a mammalian order including dolphins, porpoises, and whales.

Charadriiformes — an order of birds including shorebirds and gulls.

Chelonia — the reptile order of turtles, terrapins, and tortoises.

Chiroptera — a mammalian order including bats.

Chondrichthyes — a class of cartilaginous fish including sharks; their skeleton is made of cartilage rather than bone.

chordate — a member of phylum Chordata, possessing (at some stage in development) a notochord, a nerve cord, gill pouches, and a tail.

Ciconiiformes — an order of birds, including storks.

class — a category in the classification of living organisms (the next smaller after phylum).

classification — the process of dividing objects into related groups.

cotylosaurs — early reptiles, now extinct.

Crocodylia — the reptile order including crocodiles and alligators.

Dermoptera — a mammalian order including flying lemurs or colugos.

echolocation — sonar; a system for perceiving the environment by interpreting the patterns of echoes produced by sounds bouncing off objects; used by bats, dolphins, and whales.

Edentata — a mammalian order including anteaters, armadillos, and sloths.

Eutheria — the subclass of placental mammals.

Falconiformes — an order of day-hunting birds including eagles, hawks, and falcons.

family — a category in the classification of living organisms (the next smaller after order).

genus — a group of rather closely related organisms.

gills — organs in fish and amphibians used for breathing underwater.

gill slits — openings in the pharynx used by tunicates and lancelets to filter food.

herbivore — a plant eater.

hominids — humans and their direct ancestors.

hominoids — a group including the apes and the hominids.

Hyracoidea — a mammalian order including hyraxes.

Insectivora — insectivores; the mammalian order of insect eaters, including moles, shrews, and hedgehogs.

invertebrate — an animal without a backbone or other internal skeleton.

kingdom — the largest group in the classification of living organisms.

Lacertilia — the reptile suborder of lizards.

Lagomorpha — a mammalian order including hares, pikas, and rabbits.

lancelet — a member of subphylum Cephalochordata, primitive chordates with a fishlike body; includes Amphioxus.

lobe-finned fish — fish with both gills and lungs; ancestors of amphibians.

Mammalia — mammals; a class of vertebrates with fur that feed their young with milk.

Marsupialia — marsupials; the mammalian order whose young complete their development inside a pouch (marsupium) on the mother's abdomen.

metamorphosis — a series of startling changes an animal goes through in developing from an immature form to an adult.

Monotremata — monotremes; the mammalian order whose members lay eggs; includes echidnas and the duck-billed platypus.

notochord — a stiff rod that runs the length of an animal's body and acts as a support for its skeleton.

omnivore — an animal that eats both plants and animals.

Ophidia — the reptile suborder of snakes.

order — a category in the classification of living organisms (the next smaller after class).

Osteichthyes — a class of bony fish.

ostracoderms — extinct jawless fish with bodies covered by thick bony plates.

Passeriformes — an order of birds including finches, starlings, thrushes, and swallows.

Pelecaniformes — an order of birds including shorebirds and gulls.

Perissodactyla — odd-toed ungulates; a mammalian order including horses, rhinoceroses, and tapirs.

Pholidota — a mammalian order including pangolins.

phylum — a major category in the classification of living organisms.

Pinnipedia — a mammalian order including seals, sea lions, and walruses.

placental mammals — mammals whose young develop inside the mother's body, nourished by a placenta.

Primates — a mammalian order including monkeys, lemurs, apes, and humans.

Proboscidea — a mammalian order including elephants.

Procellariiformes — an order of birds including albatrosses.

Prosimii — prosimians; the primate suborder that includes lemurs and tarsiers.

ratite birds — flightless birds, including ostriches, rheas, emus, and kiwis.

ray-finned fish — fish with swim bladders; most of the currently living fish species.

Reptilia — reptiles; a class of vertebrates that includes lizards, snakes, turtles, alligators, and crocodiles as well as extinct dinosaurs.

Rodentia — a mammalian order including beavers, gophers, mice, rats, porcupines, and squirrels.

Sirenia — a mammalian order including dugongs and manatees.

species — a group of very closely related organisms, each able to breed with others in the group.

spinal cord — the main nerve cord that runs through the length of a vertebrate's body.

spine — the vertebral column, a long tubelike structure made of individual bones (vertebrae) held together in slightly movable joints, which provides support for body structures.

Squamata — the reptile order including snakes and lizards.

Strigiformes — an order of night-hunting birds including owls.

swim bladder — inflatable air sacs that help fish to float in the water.

taxonomy — the science of classifying or arranging living things into groups based on the characteristics they share.

Teleostei — the order including nearly all present-day fish species.

thecodonts — extinct lizardlike reptiles believed to be the ancestors of the birds.

therapsids — extinct mammal-like reptiles.

Tubulidentata — a mammalian order containing the aardvark.

tunicate — a member of subphylum Urochordata, primitive chordates whose adult form has a baglike body; includes sea squirts.

ungulates — hoofed mammals.

Urodela — the order of tailed amphibians, including salamanders and newts; also called Caudata.

vertebrate — an animal with a backbone (internal spine made of bones called vertebrae).

INDEX
